Granville Sharp

The Law of Liberty

Or, Royal law, by which all mankind will certainly be judged! Earnestly

recommended to the serious consideration of all slave holders and slave

dealers

Granville Sharp

The Law of Liberty
Or, Royal law, by which all mankind will certainly be judged! Earnestly recommended to the serious consideration of all slave holders and slave dealers

ISBN/EAN: 9783337411435

Printed in Europe, USA, Canada, Australia, Japan

Cover: Foto ©Suzi / pixelio.de

More available books at **www.hansebooks.com**

THE
LAW of LIBERTY,

OR,

ROYAL LAW,

BY WHICH

ALL MANKIND WILL CERTAINLY *BE JUDGED!*

EARNESTLY RECOMMENDED TO THE

SERIOUS CONSIDERATION

OF ALL

SLAVEHOLDERS AND *SLAVEDEALERS*.

By GRANVILLE SHARP.

" *So speak ye, and so do, as they that shall be* JUDGED
" *by* THE LAW OF LIBERTY." Jam. ii. 12.

LONDON:

Printed for B. WHITE, at Horace's Head, in Fleet Street;
and E. and C. DILLY, in the Poultry.

M DCC LXXVI.

THE

LAW OF LIBERTY,

OR,

ROYAL LAW.

IN two former Tracts I have attempted to defcribe the JUST LIMITATION OF SLAVERY IN THE LAWS OF GOD, and THE LAW OF PASSIVE OBEDIENCE, with refpect more particularly to the due SUBMISSION of *Chriftian Servants* or *Slaves* to their *Mafters*.

The purpofe of the prefent Tract is not only to point out the reciprocal duty of *Chriftian Mafters* to their *Servants,* and all other perfons with whom they are connected, but alfo more particularly

to

to enable our *British American* Slave-holders to examine or *measure* (with very little trouble) by *the Rule* of God's Holy Word, *the Legality* or *Illegality of Slavery among Christians*. For this purpose some of the clearest and most essential *Maxims* or *Principles* of Scripture are selected and compared with each other in the following pages.

" *So speak ye, and so do, as they that* " *shall be* JUDGED *by* THE LAW OF " LIBERTY."

This the earnest advice of the Apostle James in his General Epistle; (ii. 12.) and as it is therefore manifest that we shall certainly BE JUDGED by " THE " LAW OF LIBERTY," it becomes a business of the utmost importance to ascertain what particular Law is thereby to be understood, that we may *write it on our hearts*, since our everlasting happiness

pinefs depends upon it, and the peril
of eternal damnation feems to attend a
breach of it; " *for he fhall have* JUDG-
" MENT WITHOUT MERCY" (fays the
Apoftle in the following verfe) " *who*
" *hath fhewed* NO MERCY!" The neceffary premifes for the examination of
the queftion are nothing lefs than the
fundamental moral Principles of Chriftianity; and if I am rather prolix in
defining them, I hope *the importance of*
the fubject will be confidered as a fuffi-
cient excufe; for indeed *the fubject* is
not only *important* to thofe perfons for
whofe ufe this Tract is particularly intended (*I mean thofe perfons who defire to*
be fatisfied concerning THE LEGALITY
or ILLEGALITY OF SLAVERY AMONG
CHRISTIANS) but to all Mankind be-
fides of every rank and denomination.

All the moral duties of the Gofpel
are briefly comprehended in *two fingle*
Prin-

Principles of the Law of Mofes, viz. THE LOVE OF GOD, and THE LOVE OF OUR NEIGHBOUR. Nothing, therefore, can be efteemed truly *lawful* under the Gofpel, that is, in the leaft, repugnant to either of thefe; and we need never be at a lofs to diftinguifh what is, or what is not fo, if we will but carefully confider the proportion or degree of *that Love,* which is clearly expreffed to be *due,* both to *God* and our *Neighbour* in thefe two comprehenfive and eternal maxims. The degree of *Love due to God* exceeds all comparifon or confideration of other things; for it muft (fays the text) be " *with* ALL *thy heart, and with* " ALL " *thy foul, and with* ALL *thy might.*" (Deut. vi. 5.) which neceffarily implies a moft fervent zeal for the glory of GOD, far exceeding all worldly confiderations. And with refpect to the degree or true proportion of *Love due to our Neighbour,* we have no pretence to plead ignorance, fince since the appointed *measure* of it is contained in *every Man's Breaſt*—" THOU " SHALT LOVE THY NEIGHBOUR AS " THYSELF. (Lev. xix. 18.) " *On* " *theſe two Commandments*" (ſaid the Eternal Judge) " *hang* ALL THE LAW " *and* THE PROPHETS." (Mat. 22. 40.) The ſame Eternal Judge of Mankind made alſo, on another occaſion, a ſimilar declaration concerning the *Sum or Compendium* " OF THE LAW AND THE " PROPHETS"—" *All things whatſoever* " *ye would that Men ſhould do to you*" (ſaid he) " *do ye even ſo to them; for* " *this is* THE LAW AND THE PRO- " PHETS." (Matth. vii. 12.) This moſt excellent rule of conduct and behaviour towards *our Neighbours*, which includes the whole Subſtance or Spirit of " THE LAW AND THE PROPHETS," ſo perfectly correſponds with the ſecond great Commandment, to LOVE *our Neighbours as ourſelves* (viz. to manifeſt our

B   LOVE,

LOVE, *by* DOING *to them, as we ourselves might* WITH REASON AND JUSTICE *expect and desire* THEY WOULD DO UNTO US) that it seems intended like a sort of paraphrase to explain the true tenour of it; for though the mode of expression is different, yet the effect of the doctrine is undoubtedly the same; because the Apostle Paul has in like manner declared this second great Commandment to be *the Compendium of* " *all the Law."* " *All* " *the Law"* (says he) " *is fulfilled in one* " *word, even in this: Thou shalt* LOVE " *thy Neighbour* AS THYSELF." (Gal. v. 14.

SELF-LOVE, therefore, must be the RULE or MEASURE (not of Self-gratification, or private Interest, but) *of our Conduct and Behaviour towards other Men!* It must not be SOLE TENANT of the heart; but is always to leave *equal* room for a due balance of *that Love which we*

owe

owe to our Neighbour, whenever the prefent circumftances (whatever they may
be) require a confcientious regard to the
publick Good, or a fympathetick confideration for *the Feelings and Sufferings of
Individuals*, to enable us to fulfil *our
Duty to our Neighbour*. SELF-LOVE is
not hereby *excluded*; for *Self-prefervation*, and a prudent regard for our own
fupport and happinefs, may ftill be allowed an *equal Share* of our confideration, without a Breach of *this fecond great
Commandment*, which would otherwife be
too hard and difficult for *Human Nature*
to receive : we are not commanded there-
in to love our Neighbours MORE *than
ourfelves*, but only (ὡς) AS *ourfelves* ; fo
that SELF-LOVE is apparently the *true
Meafure of our Conduct and Behaviour towards other Men :* and though an exalted
Senfe of *Duty to God* (according to the
firft great Commandment) may, in fome
particular cafes, prompt Men to noble
B 2 actions,

actions, wherein SELF-LOVE may feem to be loft in a generous and benevolent regard to others (of which there are feveral inftances in Scripture, as I have elfewhere fhewn (1) ; and alfo though the like admirable generofity and perfect difintereftednefs may, poffibly, upon fome unforefeen occafion, become likewife the peculiar duty of any one of us, viz. " *to lay down* (our) *Lives for the Bre-* " *thren* (2), 1 John iii. 16. yet as this far exceeds the meafure of *Love* laid down

(1) See my Tract on *the Law of Nature, and Principles of Action in Man.* P. 79—105.

(2) *Hereby perceive we* (or rather, it fhould be rendered, *Hereby have we perceived*) " *the* LOVE (of God), " *becaufe he laid down his Life for us*" (faid the Apoftle, and then he immediately informs us of the duty which arifes from that extraordinary manifeftation of LOVE) " AND WE OUGHT (fays he) TO LAY DOWN (our) " LIVES FOR THE BRETHREN." 1 John iii. 16. This plain declaration of our duty (ἡμεῖς οφειλομεν, &c. " WE OUGHT *to lay down our Lives*," &c.) fufficiently enables us to account for the many extraordinary examples of SELF-LOVE *being fuperfeded by more noble Principles,* fome of which I have cited in my Tract on *the Law of Nature,*

down in the fecond great Commandment, which is given us as the *general*
or

Nature, and Principles of Action in Man, p. 79—105, to
which alfo the following may be added.

THE GRATITUDE of the *Galatians* to their Teacher
Paul, is expreffed by that Apoftle in the ftrongeft terms—
" *I bear you record* (fays he) *that if it had been poffible, ye*
" *would have plucked out your own eyes, and have given*
" *them to me.*" Gal. iv. 15.

Not inferior to this was the LOVE of that fame Apoftle
himfelf towards *the Corinthians,* though they were fo far
from returning a *mutual affection* like *the Galatians,* that
the Apoftle, it feems, had reafon to complain of their
INGRATITUDE—" *I will very gladly* SPEND, AND BE
" SPENT *for you* (literally " *for your Souls,*" faid he)
" *though the more abundantly I* LOVE *you, the lefs I be*
" LOVED." 2 Cor. xii. 15.

To " SPEND, AND BE SPENT" for others, and that
" *very gladly !*" is the ftrongeft expreffion of *difinterefted*
LOVE that could have been chofen ! It implies a chearful
facrifice of every thing that is dear in this world (LIFE
ITSELF NOT EXCEPTED !) " *and greater Love hath no*
" *Man than this, that a Man lay down his Life for his*
" *friends.*" John xv. 13. So that, as *no Man can have
greater Love than this,* we may certainly efteem it the
higheft demonftration of " *perfect Love ;*" and as the fentence laft quoted from the Apoftle John relates, in its pri-
mary application, to the voluntary facrifice which Chrift
made of himfelf to fave Mankind, it leads us to the true
foundation of that " *perfect Love*" enjoined in the Scriptures,

or *ordinary* Rule of Life, we may be
affured, that fuch a very difficult duty,

as

tures, which (as the preceding examples demonftrate)
does occafionally overcome the general Principle of " *Self-*
" *love*," and every other *interefted* Motive natural to
" Man !

The Apoftle John informs us, no lefs than *twice* in *one*
chapter, that " GOD IS LOVE !" (ὁ Θεος αγαπη εϛιν.
1 John iv. 8. ὁ Θεος αγαπη εϛί. ibid. v. 16.)

This information is introduced in an argument, whereby
the Apoftle endeavours to inculcate a due fenfe of the
neceffity we are laid under, *to love one another*, becaufe
God hath firft *loved us :* fo that GRATITUDE TO GOD
muft be the foundation of our " *Love to one another ;*"
and we are therefore bound to imitate (and will certainly
endeavour to imitate, if " GOD DWELLETH IN US."
See 1 John iv. 13. 16.) that glorious Attribute of the
Divine Nature, LOVE (" GOD IS LOVE") which he has
manifefted towards us, by facrificing all that could be *truly*
perfect and *dear* in his fight, even his only begotten Son,
who alfo *voluntarily fubmitted himfelf* (for our happinefs
and *eternal* welfare) to the moft fevere *temporal* fufferings,
and trials, *even unto death !*

To GOD, and to the ETERNAL WORD, therefore, (to
whom we are indebted, not only for that extraordinary
manifeftation of LOVE, but for all other things that we
enjoy, even for our very exiftence) our return of LOVE,
muft be UNLIMITED ; and the *natural Principle* of SELF-
LOVE, which is given as the meafure of our LOVE *to our*
Neighbour in the *Law of Liberty*, or *fecond great Command-*
ment,

as that of *laying down our Lives for the Brethren*, can only be required of us on very

ment, muſt be entirely ſuppreſſed whenever it falls in com-
petition with *the Love of God* enjoined in the *firſt great
Commandment* ; and though this doctrine is very hard and
difficult to be received, and much more difficult to be
practiſed, as it includes the moſt exalted *Heroiſm* and
Greatneſs of Soul that Human Nature is capable of attain-
ing, yet we have ample reaſon to hope and truſt (as the
diſcharge of our *Duty to our Neighbour* includes and fulfils
the moſt eſſential part of *our Duty to God*) that thoſe men,
who carefully endeavour to make " *the Law of Liberty*,"
(I mean *the ſecond great Commandment*) their *general* or
ordinary Rule of Conduct IN LIFE, will not want due
aſſiſtance from the Almighty to enable them to fulfil alſo
the duty which ariſes from *the firſt great Commandment*, even
UNTO DEATH, if any extraordinary emergency ſhould
require ſuch a manifeſtation of their LOVE ; becauſe we
are aſſured by the Scriptures, that " GOD *dwelleth*" in
thoſe men, who maintain the proper meaſure of *Love* and
Benevolence for the reſt of mankind.

 " BELOVED" (ſaid the *beloved* Apoſtle) " *let us* LOVE
" *one another : for* LOVE *is of* GOD, *and every one that*
" LOVETH *is born of* GOD, *and knoweth* GOD. *He that*
" LOVETH NOT *knoweth not God,* FOR GOD IS LOVE.
" *In this was manifeſted the* LOVE OF GOD *towards us,*
" *becauſe that* GOD *ſent his only begotten Son into the world,*
" *that we might live through him. Herein is* LOVE, *not*
" *that* WE LOVED GOD, *but that he* LOVED US, *and ſent*
" *his Son to be the propitiation for our ſins.* BELOVED, IF
" GOD SO LOVED US, *we ought alſo to* LOVE ONE ANO-
            " THER.

very extraordinary occafions, as in times
of perfecution, or on other fuch preffing
emergencies, when fome very fingular
Good or Benefit to our *Friends*, our
Country, or *Mankind in general*, apparently depends upon our perfeverance
unto death for their fakes, in a juft caufe
to the Glory of God; or to the manifeftation of his revealed *Truth*, for their
confirmation and example! This is, indeed, the beft and moft noble foundation, not only for true PATRIOTISM
in all Men, *as Members*, refpectively, *of
fome particular Nation*, but alfo for UNI-
VERSAL BENEVOLENCE, *as Citizens of
the World*; which latter Duty fhould
always regulate and limit the former (viz.
PATRIOTISM) by the eternal Rules of

" THER. *No man hath feen God at any time. If we love
one another*, GOD DWELLETH IN US, *and his* LOVE
" *is perfected in us.*" 1 John iv. 7—12. And again, in
the 16th verfe—" *We have known and believed the* LOVE
" *that God hath to us.* GOD IS LOVE, *and he that dwelleth*
" *in* LOVE, DWELLETH IN GOD, AND GOD IN HIM.
" *Herein is our* LOVE MADE PERFECT, &c.

natural

natural Equity and Juſtice. But though a chearful obedience in this ultimate Duty of *laying down our Lives*, and ſacrificing *Self-love*, and every temporal Bleſſing *for the Good of others*, does undoubtedly exalt HUMAN NATURE to the higheſt pitch of *Heroiſm* and *real Dignity*, let us all, nevertheleſs, pray God (as in effect we do by that comprehenſive expreſſion in our daily prayers— *" Lead us not into temptation"*) to preſerve us from any ſuch ſevere trials of our Obedience and LOVE to him as the neceſſity of of *" laying down our Lives " for the Brethren ;"* left, through the want of preſence of mind, or unwarineſs, or through weakneſs and natural infirmity, any of us ſhould unhappily ſhrink back from that ultimate Duty, and thereby incur the dreadful condemnation of thoſe that *deny Chriſt before Men !* Let us alſo be truly thankful, that the *abſolute Command*, in the

C

ſecond

fecond great Branch of our Duty, by which *all Mankind are to be* JUDGED (as fhall hereafter be fhewn) extends no farther than to limit SELF-LOVE by a fympathetick Confideration or *Fellow-feeling* for our *Neighbour's* welfare, left the former (*Self-love*) fhould be confidered as the proper and " *univerfal* " *Principle of Action,*" and thereby endanger the peace and happinefs of Society by its *partial* inftigations : let me add too, that if SELF-LOVE is not thus reftrained, it will defeat its own Purpofe and fixed Principles of *Self-prefervation,* by incurring a dreadful and eternal Doom !

The OMISSION of an Act of *Mercy* and *Benevolence* towards our Neighbour, when it is in our power, and occafion requires it, *is declared by our Lord, the Saviour of the World,* to be as grofs an affront, *even to himfelf,* as if *he* had been

perfonally

perfonally neglected and denied by us!
" *Inafmuch* (fays he) *as ye did it not to*
" *one of the leaft of thefe,* YE DID IT
" NOT TO ME." Matt. xxv. 45. And
if SINS of OMISSION, even towards *the
meaneft· of our Brethren,* are by OUR
LORD efteemed as a *perfonal Affront
to himfelf,* we may be affured, that the
actual COMMISSION of Injuries will be
infinitely more heinous in his fight, and
cannot efcape his juft Vengeance. We
muft remember alfo, that *this Declaration* of our Lord will be made to thofe
miferable wretches, who fhall ftand " *on*
" *the Left Hand,*" after the tremendous
final fentence is paffed upon them!
" *Depart from me ye Curfed, into ever-*
" *lafting Fire, prepared for the Devil*
" *and his Angels!*" See verfe 41.

It is manifeft therefore, that *a Viola-
lation of* THE LOVE THAT IS DUE TO
OUR NEIGHBOUR, is a Violation alfo of

THE

THE LOVE OF GOD; and, on the contrary, *the latter is perfected* by a ſtrict obedience *to the former*—" *If we* LOVE *one another*" (ſays *the beloved* Apoſtle) " *God dwelleth in us, and* HIS LOVE IS " PERFECTED IN US." (1 John iv. 12.) So that the two great Commandments appear to be reciprocally included and blended together in their conſequences; by which we may more readily perceive the propriety of our Lord's declaration, that the *ſecond great Commandment is like unto the firſt* (3); and this reciprocal connexion between them enables us alſo to comprehend the reaſon why *the ſecond is given alone* (when BOTH are undoubtedly neceſſary) as the grand teſt of Chriſtian obedience, and as the ſum and eſ-

---

(3) " *Thou ſhalt love the Lord thy God with all thy* " *heart, and with all thy ſoul, and with all thy mind.* " *This is the firſt and great Commandment.* AND THE " SECOND IS LIKE UNTO IT, *Thou ſhalt love thy Neigh-* " *bour as thyſelf. On theſe two Commandments hang all* " *the Law and the Prophets.*" (Matt. xxii. 37. to 40.)

ſtian

fence of the whole Law of God. *" For
" all the Law is fulfilled"* (fays the Apoſtle
Paul) *" in one word,* (even) *in this, Thou
" ſhalt love thy Neighbour as thyſelf."*
(Gal. v. 14.)

Now a continued multiplication of
Statutes (as in England, where the number exceeds the capacity of the human
Memory) affords matter only for *Equi-
vocation, Doubt,* and *Evaſion,* whereby
SOUND LAW is vitiated and corrupted;
and the loathſome *Proſtitute,* ſtill retain-
ing *the Name of* LAW, *ariſes* (like the
Harlot POPERY from pure CHRISTI-
ANITY) *in another Dreſs!* She is clothed
with the many-coloured garment of mif-
conſtruction, and feats herſelf at the
right hand of the unjuſt judge, prompt-
ing him with wily Subterfuges, and *bad
Precedents* inſtead of LAW; whereby he
is enabled to enſnare the innocent, and
ſcreen the guilty. But, on the other hand,
when we conſider that " ALL LAW" is
reduced

reduced to so small a compass, that it
may be accounted, comparatively, as ONE
WORD, there is no room left for offenders to plead *Ignorance,* as an excuse for
having violated the general Laws of
Morality, and the *natural Rights of Mankind.* Let me therefore exhort my op-
ponents, as they regard their own eternal welfare, to take this subject into
their most serious consideration, and no
longer refuse to acknowledge this glorious WORD or *Maxim,* as the TRUE
MEASURE (except a still greater measure
of LOVE is required (4) of all their actions,
and more especially with respect to the
present point before us, the *Legality or
Illegality of Slavery among Christians!* For
this question, by infallible necessity,
falls under the decision of *this very
Law;* because it sets before us our own
personal Feelings, as *the proper Measure
or Standard of our Behaviour to other*

(4) This exception relates only to such extraordinary
cases of emergency as are mentioned in pages 12 to 17.

Men;

Men; for Tyrants, Slaveholders, Extortioners, and other Oppreffors, would moft certainly diflike to be treated as as they treat others; fo that this compendious Law neceffarily excludes *the leaft. Toleration of Slavery*, or of any other *Oppreffion*, which an *innocent Man* (5) would be unwilling to experience in his own perfon from another.

We

(5) On the other hand, *notorious offenders*, that are clearly convicted of their crimes by the laws of the land, may, confiftently *with reafon and juftice*, be punifhed with a temporary DEPRIVATION OF LIBERTY, provided they be not *fold to ftrangers*, nor even to *their own countrymen*, to be fubjected to *private dominion*, or the *abfolute rule of individuals*, which is dreadfully baneful to morality! The community at large (and *that community only whofe Laws they have broken*) can alone have any RIGHT to detain them in *bondage*; and this RIGHT of detaining fhould be moderated by fuch wholefome regulations for the religious *inftruction*, as well as *employment*, of the unhappy convicts, as fhould apparently tend more to their *reformation*, (to render them worthy of being fpeedily reftored to *Liberty*) than to any other object; and no perfons whatfoever fhould be entrufted with the care, inftruction, or employment of fuch *public delinquents*, without being fubject to the infpection and *legal* controul of the king's judges, and of other regular *crown officers* of the *Law department* (but of no other *crown officers* as fuch whatever) as alfo of the county courts of affizes and feffions,

courts

We muſt therefore acknowledge this heavenly maxim to be the true ſtandard, not only of *mutual Benevolence* among MEN, but alſo, of *our Love and Duty* to GOD ; ſince it includes the firſt great Commandment, by " *perfecting the Love* " *of God in us,*" as I have before remarked (ſee p. 20.); ſo that it muſt neceſſarily be eſteemed the moſt ſure and beſt foundation " of PERFECT LIBERTY." And accordingly we find it expreſſly diſtinguiſhed in Scripture by the title of " *the Law of Liberty.*"

" *So ſpeak ye, and ſo do,*" (ſays the Apoſtle James) " *as they that ſhall be* " *judged by* THE LAW OF LIBERTY." (James ii. 12.) This title properly belongs, indeed, to the *whole Law,* or

courts of inqueſt, grand juries, juſtices of the peace, ſheriffs, and of ſuch other *legal* guardians of the public peace, for and in behalf of the public, leſt the cauſe of *liberty* ſhould ſuffer by the influence of any innovation in that reſpect.

Goſpel

Gospel of Christ, and seems to be so applied by the same Apostle in the preceding chapter (25th verse) wherein he
speaks of " *the perfect* LAW OF LIBER-
" TY."—Yet the *general* application of
the title does not lessen the propriety of
that *particular* application, which I conceive to have been intended by the
Apostle in this 2d chapter, because the
precept in question is *a complete Compendium of Christian Morality*, containing
(as I have before observed) the *very
Essence of the whole Gospel*, or *general*
LAW OF LIBERTY, with respect to our
Duty towards Men, and has, therefore,
an indisputable Right, also, to the *general Title of the whole*. But there are
other reasons to justify the application
of this *general Title of the Gospel* to that
one comprehensive *Word*, or Maxim, in
which " *all the Law is fulfilled*."—
Though the Apostle James seems to
mean the *whole Gospel* in that passage of

D   his

his firſt chapter, wherein he mentions
" THE PERFECT LAW OF LIBERTY."
—Yet the whole tenor of his argument
in the 2d chapter, where he again mentions THE LAW OF LIBERTY, is apparently founded on the Principles of
the glorious Maxim in queſtion——
" THOU SHALT LOVE THY NEIGH-
" BOUR AS THYSELF;" for the *Subject*,
in the beginning of the chapter, particularly relates to *the Duty we owe to* OUR
NEIGHBOURS, being a warning againſt
" *Reſpect of Perſons*," or *Partiality* ; and
as the Maxim in queſtion forbids even
Self-preference, by directing us *to* " *love*
" *our Neighbours* (ὡς) AS *ourſelves*," it is ſo
apparently ſuitable to the Apoſtle's *ſub-*
ject, that he expreſſly cites it under the
eminent title of the " *Royal Law* (νομον
Βασιλικον) to enforce his argument. " *My*
" *Brethren*" (ſays he) " *have not the*
" *Faith of our Lord Jeſus Chriſt*" (the
Lord) " *of Glory*, WITH RESPECT OF
                                    " PER-

" PERSONS ;" and then, after charging
them in the 2d and 3d verses with *Partiality*, in *preferring* a well-dreffed Man
in their affemblies to the *Poor*, and after
appealing to them thereupon in the 4th
and 5th verses, faying, " *Are ye not*
" *partial in yourfelves*," &c. and alfo,
after reproving them (in the 6th and 7th
verfes) for *defpifing the Poor* ; he adds,
in the 8th verfe—" *If ye fulfil*," (fays he)
" *the* ROYAL LAW (νομον Βασιλικον) *according to the Scripture*, THOU SHALT
" LOVE THY NEIGHBOUR AS THY-
" SELF," (which is the very Maxim in
queftion) " *ye do well: But if ye have*
" RESPECT TO PERSONS," (fays he,
thereby plainly pointing out this PAR-
TIALITY as a direct breach of the faid
ROYAL LAW) " *ye commit Sin, and are*
" *convinced of the Law as Tranfgreffors.*
For whofoever fhall keep the whole Law,"
(continues the Apoftle) *and yet offend in*
" *one* (point) *he is guilty of all. For he*
" *that*

" *that said do not commit Adultery; said*
" *also, Do not kill. Now if thou commit*
" *no Adultery, yet if thou kill, thou art*
" *become a Transgressor of the Law. So*
" *speak ye, and so do ye, as they that shall*
" *be* JUDGED *by the* LAW OF LIBERTY,"
(manifestly referring us to the *indispen-*
sible Principle of doing as we would be done
by, or to that which is exactly parallel
—*the loving our Neighbours as ourselves*)
" FOR HE SHALL HAVE JUDGMENT
" WITHOUT MERCY" (said the Apostle)
" THAT HATH SHEWED NO MERCY;
" *and Mercy rejoiceth against Judgment.*"
(James ii, 1. to 13.)

This absolute necessity that we are
laid under *to shew Mercy, that we may
obtain Mercy,* is apparently founded on
the very same *Principle,* which our Lord
declared to be ' *the Law and the Pro-
' phets ;*' that is, the sum and essence of
the whole Scriptures, as I have before
remarked

remarked—" ALL THINGS WHATSO-
" EVER YE WOULD THAT MEN SHOULD
" DO TO YOU, DO YE EVEN SO TO
" THEM: FOR THIS IS THE LAW AND
" THE PROPHETS;" (Mat. vii. 12.)
and I have already shewn (in p. 3.)
that this comprehensive Maxim is exactly
the same in effect (though expressed in
different words) as the second great
Commandment of our Lord, " THOU
" SHALT LOVE THY NEIGHBOUR AS
" THYSELF;" in which (as the Apostle
Paul has expressly declared) " *All the*
" *Law is fulfilled,*" viz. " *All the Law*
(says he) " *is fulfilled in* ONE WORD (even)
" *in this,* THOU SHALT LOVE THY
" NEIGHBOUR AS THYSELF." (Gal.
v. 14.)

This *one Word* (as the Maxim is
esteemed by the Apostle Paul) is therefore undoubtedly that glorious " LAW
" OF LIBERTY" by which *we shall all*
be

be judged, as the Apoſtle James hath fairly warned us—" *So ſpeak ye, and ſo* " *do*" (ſays he) " *as they that* SHALL " BE JUDGED BY THE LAW OF LI- " BERTY." And therefore, if what has already been ſaid be duly conſidered, the propriety of citing this glorious and comprehenſive LAW OF LIBERTY, in vindication of the NATURAL LIBERTY OF MANKIND *againſt the Tyranny of Slaveholders,* cannot be doubted or called in queſtion; for though this SUPREME LAW virtually prohibits every other kind of *Oppreſſion,* yet its very title leads us to a more particular and expreſs appli- cation of it AGAINST THE TOLERA- TION OF SLAVERY AMONG CHRISTI- ANS: becauſe it ſeems to be thus emi- nently diſtinguiſhed by the appointment of God himſelf in his Holy Word, as *the peculiar Antidote* againſt that *baneful Evil* (SLAVERY) which is moſt oppoſite and repugnant to its glorious title— " THE

" THE LAW OF LIBERTY." This
" LAW OF LIBERTY," this SUPREAM,
this " ROYAL LAW," muſt therefore
be our guide in the interpretation and
examination of all Laws which relate
to the Rights of Perſons, becauſe it ex‑
cludes *Partiality,* or *Reſpect of Perſons,*
and conſequently removes all ground for
the pretence of any *abſolute Right of Do‑
minion inherent in the Maſters* over their
Slaves : for as all Ranks of Men are
EQUAL *in the Sight of God* (the Chriſtian
Slave, or Servant, being *the Freeman* of
the Lord, and the Chriſtian *Maſter* the
Servant of Chriſt, 1 Cor. vii. 22.) there
is no doubt but that the ſame *Chriſtian*
Qualities are neceſſary to be maintained
by the *Chriſtian* MASTER, that are re‑
quired of the *Chriſtian* SERVANT ; as
Humility, Forgiveneſs of Treſpaſſes or
Debts, and (though not *Submiſſion,* yet
certainly) *Brotherly Love towards Infe‑
riors,* with *unfeigned Charity* and *univer‑*
ſal

fal Benevolence, founded on the glorious Maxim, or *Royal Law,* " THOU SHALT " LOVE THY NEIGHBOUR AS THY- " SELF." All which are as indifpenfably neceffary to form the difpofition of a *true Chriftian Mafter,* as they are abfo- lutely incompatible with the oppreffive and tyrannical Claims of our American Slaveholders! *" Quod tibi fieri non vis,* " *alteri ne feceris. What thou wouldeft* " *not have done to thee, do not thou to* " *another,"*—was the favourite Maxim of the Emperor *Alexander Severus,* ac- cording to the Report of *Lampridius* quoted by the learned Jof. Mede, Book 3. p. 550. This Principle was probably deduced from " THE ROYAL LAW," " or LAW OF LIBERTY;" for *Lam- pridius* relates, that the Emperor heard it either from fome Jews or Chriftians: (" *Quod à quibufdam five Judæis five* " *Chriftianis audierat, et tenebat,"* &c.) and

and it cannot be denied, that the doctrine
of it is neceffarily included in that great
and indifpenfable Commandment. The
doctrine was expreffed even by Chrift
himfelf nearly to the fame effect, which
I have already quoted :—" *All things*
" *whatfoever ye would that Men fhould do*
" *to you, do ye even fo to them :* FOR THIS
" IS THE LAW *and* THE PROPHETS."
(Mat. vii. 12.) So that Slavery is abfolutely inconfiftent with Chriftianity,
becaufe we cannot fay of any *Slaveholder*,
that he *doth not* to another, what he
would not have done to himfelf! For
he is continually exacting *involuntary
Labour* from others *without Wages*,
which he would think monftroufly unjuft, were he himfelf the Sufferer!
Nay, many of them are fo befotted
with Avarice, that they are not content
with reaping *the whole Fruit of other
Men's Labour upon Earth* WITHOUT

E   WAGES;

WAGES (3); but would deprive their
poor Labourers even of their *eternal
Comfort*, if they could exact a little
more Work from them, by reducing
them nearer to the State of Brutes!—
What I advance cannot be denied; for
it is notorious, that *many Masters* oppose
the instruction of their *Slaves* in Christian Knowledge; and *but very few* pro-
mote it as they ought; so that the Iniquity of the ignorant Slave must rest *with
double Weight* on the guilty head of the
owner, to fill up the measure of his sins!

Suppose a reverse of fortune—that
an English or Scotch *Slaveholder*, or
Slavedealer, is shipwrecked on the Bar-
bary Coast, and is retained, *as a Slave,*
by the Moors, who seize him; or is
sold, as such, to another Person, accord-

(3) " *Woe unto him that buildeth his House by Unright-*
" *eousness, and his Chambers by Wrong; that* USETH HIS
" NEIGHBOUR'S SERVICE WITHOUT WAGES, AND
" GIVETH HIM NOT FOR HIS WORK." Jer. xxii. 13.

ing

ing to the deteftable cuftoms of that
Savage people!—Would he efteem himfelf the *lawful Property* of his tawney
Mafter, becaufe the wretched police of
thofe Barbarians, *in tolerating Slavery*, is
fimilar to his own former practices as
an *American Slaveholder*, or *African
Trader?* Would he not think it cruel
treatment to be efteemed *a mere Chattel*;
and, as fuch, to be ranked with the
horfes and oxen of his African Mafter?
Like them, to be compelled by ftripes
to perform the moft fervile and abject
Labour? *Like them*, to receive *no Wages*,
or other *Reward* for his Service, except
a little *coarfe Provender*, merely to keep
him in working Order for his Mafter's
Benefit? Would he not think himfelf
grievoufly injured by being forcibly detained and prevented from working for
himfelf? And would he not think himfelf abfolutely *robbed of the Fruits of his
own Labour?* He would certainly have

ample

ample reafon to lament the Mahome-
tan's Ignorance of the heavenly Precept,
" THOU SHALT LOVE THY NEIGH-
BOUR AS THYSELF ; for he would then
be taught, by his own Sufferings, to
comprehend the full force, extent, and
and meaning of that benevolent Command, which, in his profperity, he was
never *willing* to underftand, though the
doctrine is fo plain and obvious, that
there can be no excufe for mifunder-
ftanding it ; for unlefs the Slaveholder
can make it appear, *that his* SLAVE *is
not his* NEIGHBOUR, he muft neceffarily
acknowledge *this* " LAW OF LIBERTY"
to be *the true Meafure* of his conduct
and behaviour *towards his* SLAVE, as
well as *towards all other* MEN !

Let not *Slaveholders* or *African Traders*
conceive, that they are at liberty to
receive or reject this glorious Precept,
according as it may fuit their intereft

or

or convenience! But rather let them carefully examine (for they are particularly interested in the determination of the question) whether obedience to the doctrine of the great " LAW OF LIBER-" TY," is not absolutely indispensable? And whether the violation of it is not dangerous to salvation?

If they think there is any room to flatter themselves, that they do not offend God by tolerating Slavery among them, let them but examine their Actions by this " ROYAL LAW," and they will clearly perceive both their *Guilt and Danger, unless they have Consciences seared with a hot Iron!"*

" *If ye have respect unto Persons*" (says the Apostle James, when he enforces the Observation of the ROYAL LAW) " *ye* " *commit Sin, and are convinced of* THE " LAW AS TRANSGRESSORS," &c. ii. 9.

Now

Now this Offence of " *having Respect* " *unto Persons*," is a mark which strongly characterizes *Slaveholders* as Violaters of " THE ROYAL LAW."

They are courteous, friendly, and hospitable enough, in general, to Persons *of their own Rank,* as, indeed, they ought to be ; but, at the same time, they look down upon their *Slaves* (who are *equally their Brethren*) as if they were *not Human Beings,* and rank them as *mere Chattels* with their Horses and Dogs ; so that there needs no Argument to prove them guilty of " *having Respect* " *unto Persons*" in a most notorious degree, whereby they surely " *commit Sin*," and are " *convinced of the Law as Transf-* " *gressors.*" What therefore have such Men to expect, when they shall be judged by " THE LAW OF LIBERTY !" especially as the Apostle adds, " *they* " *shall*

" *ſhall have Judgment without Mercy,*
" *that have ſhewed no Mercy !*" &c.

And even our Lord himſelf has declared the very ſame doctrine, though
in different Words—" *With the ſame*
" MEASURE *that ye* METE" (ſays he)
" *ſhall it be* MEASURED *unto you again.*"
Τῳ γαϱ αυτῳ μετϱῳ ῳ μετϱειῖε αιτιμετϱηθησεται ὑμιν.
Luke vi. 38. Mat. vii. 2. Mark iv. 24.

What MEASURE of *Benevolence,* therefore, have theſe Men to expect, who
endeavour to enrich THEMSELVES by *en-*
ſlaving and *oppreſſing* their BRETHREN?
For Men, who, " *without Mercy,*" or
Fellow-feeling, have violated " THE
" ROYAL LAW OF LIBERTY," can
neither be ſaid to *love* God, nor *their*
Neighbour, as directed in the two great
Commandments, and conſequently are
Violaters of " *the whole Law ;*" by which
they abſolutely deprive themſelves of
the

the Benefit of Chrift's Redemption!
This feems to be the neceffary meaning
of that dreadful Doom before-men-
tioned ; " *He fhall have* JUDGMENT
" *without* MERCY, that *hath fhewed* NO
" MERCY."

But let no Man conceive, that I pre-
fume to charge Individuals, or *any Perfon in particular,* with the want of this
MERCY, fo neceffary to Salvation, even
though they are apparently guilty of
that oppreffive treatment of their *Neighbour,* which I now oppofe ; for this
would feem like fetting bounds to the
Mercy of God, whereby I fhould be liable
to involve myfelf, as an *uncharitable
Judge,* in the fame condemnation. And
there are, certainly, a variety of circumftances, beyond the reach of human
knowledge, that may extenuate the guilt
of *particular Perfons,* of which the great
Searcher of Hearts alone can judge!

It

It is not, therefore, *the Perfons*, but *the uncharitable Practices* of Slaveholders and Slavedealers, that I now venture *to condemn*; and thefe I can with confidence affirm to be really *damnable*, or *dangerous to Salvation*, as being the moft notorious violations of that Chriftian Charity, or LOVE OF OUR NEIGHBOUR, which God indifpenfably requires of us, and without which, the higheft Gifts are vain, and even *Faith itfelf!* For, *tho' I have* " ALL FAITH" (faid the Apoftle Paul) " *fo that I could remove Mountains, and have* " *no* CHARITY, *I am nothing.*" 1 Cor. xiii. 2. The nature of this indifpenfable CHARITY is more particularly defcribed by the fame Apoftle under the appellation of LOVE (ἡ αγαπη). " LOVE," (fays he) " *worketh no* ILL *to his Neighbour : there-* " *fore* LOVE *is the fulfilling of the Law.*" Rom. xiii. 10. But, as the being detained in *an involuntary Slavery* is one of the greateft ILLS, or EVILS, that can

happen

happen to *our Neighbour*, it muſt neceffarily be allowed, that he who *cauſes*, or
continues ſuch an *unnatural Oppreſſion* of
poor unfortunate *Strangers*, who never
injured him, nor his, nor ever voluntarily contracted to ſerve him, even for
the ſhorteſt term, much leſs for life;
ſuch a Man, I ſay, moſt certainly
" *worketh* ILL *to his Neighbour ;*" and,
confequently, violates that *ſaving* LOVE,
which is required for " *the fulfilling of*
" *the Law.*" For " *he that* LOVETH
" *another*" (ſays the Apoſtle in a preceding verfe of the fame chapter) " *hath*
" *fulfilled the Law :*" and after repeating
the feveral Articles of the Decalogue,
refpecting *our Duty towards our* NEIGH-
BOUR, he adds, " *and if there be any*
" *other Commandment, it is briefly com-*
" *prehended in this,* THOU SHALT LOVE
" THY NEIGHBOUR AS THYSELF."
Rom. xiii. 8—10. We may therefore
fairly conclude, that this glorious MAX-

IM

IM is the touchſtone or proof of *that
ſaving* LOVE, which is THE FULFILL-
ING OF THE LAW, and without which
" FAITH IS DEAD," as declared by *the
Apoſtle Paul* ; that it is alſo " THE
ROYAL LAW," being thus eminently
diſtinguiſhed from all other Precepts of
the Goſpel, by the *Apoſtle James* ; and
if it *is not* alſo particularly ſignified
(though I am fully convinced that it *is*)
under the Title of " THE LAW OF
" LIBERTY," by the *ſame Apoſtle,* in
his 2d Chapter ; yet it is ſurely one of
the moſt eſſential and comprehenſive
Principles of that " LAW OF LIBERTY,"
by which *we ſhall all be judged* ; becauſe the Apoſtle at the ſame time de-
clares, that " *he ſhall have Judgment*
WITHOUT MERCY, *who hath ſhewed* NO
MERCY ;" (chap. ii. 13.) by which he
manifeſtly refers to the Breach of that
particular Precept, which ought to regulate the Conduct of all Mankind to-

wards each other; and therefore, laftly,
we muft acknowledge this fame Precept
to be alfo THE TRUE MEASURE or Teft
on which our eternal Doom will depend
in that awful Day, when it " *fhall be*
" MEASURED *unto us again," according
to* THE MEASURE of our Actions, as
declared by the *eternal Judge himfelf*,
(Mat. vii. 2. Mark iv. 24. Luke vi. 38.)
whofe Words cannot fail! And if even
a mere *Neglect* or *Omiffion* in our Duty
towards our *Neighbour* is fo *offenfive* to
our bleffed Lord, that he efteems it as
a Denial and Affront to his *own Perfon,*
(which I have already obferved) how
much more offenfive to him muft be *the
actual Commiffion* of the groffeft Injuries,
fuch as the Exaction of *an involuntary
Service* from our poor Brethren " WITH-
" OUT WAGES," and the various Cru-
elties ufually practifed to enforce the
fame, which are the neceffary and un-
avoidable Attendants on *Slavery*—What
a dreadful

a dreadful MEASURE of RETRIBUTION, then, may obstinate and unrepenting *Slaveholders* and *Slavedealers* justly expect from the righteous Judge! Surely there is but too much Cause to apprehend, that Christ will one Day PROFESS UNTO THEM—" *Inasmuch as ye have done it unto* " *one of the least of these my Brethren,* " *ye have* DONE IT UNTO ME!" (Mat. XXV. 40.)

This Sentence, indeed, is applied in the Text to those who shall have DONE GOOD to their Brethren; yet by necessary Consequence it is equally applicable (as in the 45th verse) to those who have neglected, or shewn them *no Brotherly* LOVE and CHARITY!—" *Inasmuch* (said our Lord) " *as ye did it not to one of* " *the least of these, ye did it not to me.* " *And these* (by which our Lord plainly referred to all that should neglect or violate that indispensible *Brotherly Love* and

and *Charity* which he enjoined) " *fhall*
" *go away* INTO EVERLASTING PU-
" NISHMENT : *but the Righteous into*
" *Life eternal!*"

But alas !—to *worldly* minded Men
the Judgments of *another World* feem
too far diftant to awaken their Atten-
tion, though they are liable to be called
away, in the very next Hour, to a State
of Exiftence, wherein the moft pun-
gent Remorfe will avail them nothing!
From fuch therefore, and from thofe
unrepenting Individuals, that will ftill
perfift in violating the LAW OF LIBERTY
by *Slave-dealing* and *Slave-holding*, it is
time to turn away! I have already be-
ftowed too much labour upon them, I
mean, with refpect to themfelves! But
this Warning was not intended for them
alone ;—the whole Community—every
Individual (without excepting even thofe
who never had the leaft Concern in pro-
moting

moting *Slavery*) is perfonally interefted
in the. Confideration of this Subject!
For if a Breach of God's Command,
even in the *hidden* Crime of a fingle Individual, as in the Cafe of *Achan*, could
involve a whole Nation in Trouble (4),
and deprive them of God's Blefling,
how

(4) " —*For Achan the Son of Carmi*,"—*took of* THE
" ACCURSED THING," (i. e. of that which was *devoted
to Deſtruction* by God's exprefs Command) : " *And the*
" *Anger of the Lord was kindled againſt the Children of*
" *Iſrael*." Joſhua vii. 1.—Thus the whole NATION was
involved in the Confequences of Achan's Guilt! Nay,
Jehovah himfelf exprefsly imputed the Action of that one
Individual to the NATION at large, until a folemn and
public Exertion of NATIONAL Juftice had expiated that
prefumptive Breach of his Command! For when Joſhua
and the Elders of Ifrael lay proftrate before God, lament-
ing the public Calamity and Difgrace, which a late Defeat of their Army had brought upon the NATION,—
" *the Lord* (Jehovah) *ſaid unto Joſhua, Get thee up* ;
" *wherefore lieſt thou thus upon thy Face ?* ISRAEL *hath*
" *ſinned, and* THEY HAVE *alſo* TRANSGRESSED *my Cove-*
" *nant which I commanded them : for* THEY *have even taken*
" *of* THE ACCURSED THING, *and have ſtolen*, (that is,
THEY *have ſtolen* גנבו) " *and* THEY *have diſſembled*
" *alſo, and* THEY *have put* (it) *even among their own*
" *Stuff*." (Yet this general Crime, for fo it was imputed,
was

how much more hateful in the Sight
of God muſt be a *public* Infringement
of his ROYAL LAW, THE PERFECT
LAW OF LIBERTY, by *national* Authority!

The AFRICAN SLAVE TRADE, which
includes the moſt contemptuous Violations of *Brotherly Love* and *Charity* that
men can be guiltyof, is openlyencouraged
and promoted by the Britiſh Parliament!
And the moſt deteſtable and oppreſſive

was perpetrated by *a ſingle Individual,* though the *whole*
NATION was doomed to ſuffer for it, till the actual Ag-
greſſor ſhould be brought to *public Juſtice ;* and this ſhould
teach us, that the Welfare of NATIONS greatly depends
on a ſtrict Adminiſtration of public *Juſtice* and *Righteouſ-*
neſs, leſt the State ſhould be accountable for the Crimes of
Individuals.) " *Therefore the Children of Iſrael*" (ſaid
Jehovah himſelf) " *could not ſtand before their Enemies,*
" (but) *turned* (their) *Backs before their Enemies, becauſe*
" *they were* ACCURSED." (Thus the CURSE was tranſ-
ferred to the People from THE ACCURSED THING, until
public Juſtice could trace and transfer it to the devoted
Head of the guilty Perſon !) " *Neither will I* (ſaid Jehovah) " *be with you any more, except ye deſtroy* THE
" ACCURSED *from among you.*" See the whole Chapter.

Slavery,

Slavery, that ever difgraced even the unenlightened Heathens, is notorioufly *tolerated* in the Britifh Colonies by the *public Acts* of their refpective Affemblies, —by Acts that have been ratified with the Affent and Concurrence of BRITISH KINGS!

The horrible Guilt therefore, which is incurred by *Slave-dealing* and *Slave-holding*, is no longer confined to the few hardened *Individuals*, that are immediately concerned in thofe baneful Practices, but alas! the WHOLE BRITISH EMPIRE is involved!

By the unhappy Concurrence of *National Authority*, the GUILT is rendered *National*; and *National* GUILT muft inevitably draw down from GOD fome tremendous *National* Punifhment (which, I truft, is fully demonftrated in my Tract on THE LAW of RETRIBUTION) if we do not fpeedily " *take away the accurfed*

G   " *Thing*

" *Thing from among us,*"—if we do not
carefully reform and redrefs at leaft every
public and notorious Violation of God's
" *Royal Law,*" " *the perfect Law of*
" *Liberty !*"

GRANVILLE SHARP.

" Glory to God in the Higheft !
" And on Earth—Peace,
" Good Will towards Men !"

TEXTS OF SCRIPTURE

QUOTED OR ILLUSTRATED

IN THE FOREGOING TRACT.

G 2   ROMANS.

INDEX.

I N D E X.

A

AFRICAN Slave-trade, encouraged by parliament, page 48.

Alexander Severus (emp.) his favourite maxim, 32

Author, his defign in this tract, 5. And for whofe ufe it is intended, 7. The confideration of which every man is interefted in, 7. 46. & feq. See *Slaveholders*.

B

Benevolence (univerfal) its beft foundation, 16.

Brethren, the duty of laying down our lives for them explained, 12, & feq. The higheft demonftration of perfect love, 13 *note*. Only required on very extraordinary occafions, 16.

C

Charity, an indifpenfable duty, 41.

Chriftian Mafter, his qualifications, 32.

Corinthians, their ingratitude to St. Paul, 13 *note*.

G

Galatians, their gratitude to St. Paul, 13 *note*.

GOD, the extent of our love to him, 8. Is love, 14 *note*. Our love to him perfected by that to our neighbour, 20. All men equal in his fight, 31.

Gofpel, its moral duties comprehended in two fingle principles, 7. Is properly the law of liberty, 24, & feq.

Gratitude to God, the foundation of our love to one another, 14 *note*. See *Self-love*.

J.

R.

R

F I N I S.

[58]

Tracts by the same AUTHOR.

Printed for B. WHITE, at HORACE's-HEAD,
FLEET-STREET.

I. A Short Treatife on the Englifh Tongue. Being an Attempt to render the Reading and Pronunciation of the fame more eafy to Foreigners. 1767.

II. Remarks on feveral very important Prophecies, firft Edition, in 1768, (fecond Edition, 1775.)

This Book contains, 1ft, Remarks on the Prophecy of Ifaiah vii. 13-16.—That *a Virgin fhould conceive and bear a Son.* 2dly, Remarks on the Nature and Style of prophetical Writings. 3dly, Remarks on the Accomplifhment of Ifaiah's Prophecy, (vii. 8.) " *Within threefcore and five Years fhall Ephraim be broken, that it* " *be not a People.*"—4thly, On the Departure of the *Sceptre* and *Lawgiver* from Judah. 5thly, A Confirmation of the above Remarks by farther Examples drawn from the Prophets, &c.

III. A Reprefentation of the Injuftice and dangerous Tendency of *Tolerating Slavery*; or of admitting the leaft Claim of *Private Property in the Perfons of Men* IN ENGLAND. Being an Anfwer to an Opinion, given in the Year 1729, by the (then) Attorney General and Solicitor General, concerning the Cafe of *Slaves* in GREAT-BRITAIN. 1769.

This Tract contains many Examples of the monftrous *Iniquity* and *Injuftice* of the Plantation Laws refpecting Slaves; as alfo fome Account of the gradual Abolition of the ancient Englifh *Slavery* called VILLENAGE, which was at length happily effected by the Wifdom and Perfeverance of the Englifh Courts of Common Law.

IV. Remarks concerning the Encroachments on the River Thames near *Durham-Yard.* 17-1.

V.

V. An Appendix to the Reprefentation of the Injuftice
and dangerous Tendency of tolerating Slavery.
(See Number III.) 1772.

VI. Remarks on the Opinions of fome of the moft
celebrated Writers on CROWN LAW, refpecting the
due Diftinction between *Manflaughter* and *Murder*;
fhewing that the Indulgence allowed by the Courts
to *voluntary Manflaughter* in Rencounters, DUELS,
&c. is *indifcriminate* and without Foundation in Law;
and is alfo one of the principal Caufes of the Conti-
nuance and prefent Increafe of the *bafe* and *difgrace-
ful* Practice of DUELLING. 1773.

The peculiar Cafe of *Gentlemen in the Army*, refpecting the Practice
of DUELLING, is carefully examined in this Tract; as alfo the
Depravity and Folly of *modern Men of Honour* falfely fo called.

VII. In two Parts. 1. A Declaration of the People's
Natural Right to a Share in the Legiflature; which
is the fundamental Principle of *the Britifh Conftitu-
tion of State*. 2. A Declaration, or Defence, of the
the fame Doctrine, when applied *particularly* to THE
PEOPLE OF IRELAND. 1774. (2d Edition, 1775.)

In thefe two Pieces many Examples and Proofs are produced concerning
the parliamentary Rights of the People; viz. That the Affent of the
People is abfolutely neceffary to render Laws *valid*: That a *free*
and *equal* Reprefentation of the Inhabitants of this Kingdom is
neceffary for the *Salvation* of the State, and the Security of *Peace*
and of *Property*: That the Reprefentatives of the People have no *legal*
Right to give affent in any " *new Device without Conference with*
" *their Countries*:" That it is an ancient and juft Right of the
People to elect a *new* Parliament " *every Year once, and more often*
" *if Need be*;" and that no Regulations whatfoever, wherein the
Reprefentatives are made *Judges of their own Elections*, can be ef-
fectual againft national Corruption! Examples are likewife here
given of feveral *furreptitious* STATUTES that are void through
the Want of *due legal Affent*; and of Others that are *void* by being
unjuft

unjuſt and repugnant to *conſtitutional Principles!* The Danger of keep-
ing *ſtanding Armies* is alſo demonſtrated, and the Wickedneſs and
Impolicy of Acting by *national Corruption!* &c. &c.

The following Tracts by the ſame AUTHOR
ARE
Printed for B. WHITE, in FLEET-STREET, and
E. and C. DILLY, in the POULTRY.

VIII. The juſt Limitation of *Slavery* in the *Laws of
God*, compared with the unbounded Claims of *the
African Traders* and *Britiſh American Slave-holders*.

To this Piece is added a copious Appendix, containing, An Anſwer
to the Rev. Mr. *Thompſon's* Tract in Favour of the *African Slave-
Trade*. Letters concerning *the lineal Deſcent of the Negroes* from the
Sons of HAM. The *Spaniſh* Regulations for the gradual Enfranchiſement of Slaves. A Propoſal, on the ſame Principles, for
the gradual Enfranchiſement of Slaves in *America*. REPORTS of
Determinations in the ſeveral COURTS OF LAW againſt Slavery, &c.
1776.

IX. THE LAW *of* PASSIVE OBEDIENCE; or Chriſtian
Submiſſion to perſonal Injuries :

Wherein is ſhewn that the ſeveral Texts of Scripture, which command
the entire Submiſſion of *Servants* or *Slaves* to their *Maſters*, cannot
authorize the *latter to exact an involuntary Servitude*, nor in the
leaſt Degree juſtify the Claims of modern *Slave-holders*; and alſo
that the ſeveral Texts, which enjoin *Submiſſion* to *Rulers, Magiſtrates,*
&c. do not in any Reſpect authorize the dangerous Doctrine of *an
unlimited paſſive Obedience.*

X. " THE LAW OF LIBERTY ;" or (as it is called in
Scripture *by way of Eminence)* " the *Royal Law*,"
by which *all Mankind* will certainly *be judged!*

XI.

XI. THE LAW OF RETRIBUTION ; or a ſerious Warning to *Great-Britain* and her *Colonies*, founded on unqueſtionable Examples of GOD's temporal Vengeance
againſt Tyrants, Slave-holders, and Oppreſſors.
1776.

The Examples are ſelected from Predictions, in the Old-Teſtament,
of *national* Judgements, which (being compared with the actual
Accompliſhment) demonſtrate " the ſure Word of Prophecy," as
well as the immediate Interpoſition of divine Providence, to re-
. compence impenitent *Nations* according to their Works.

Tracts, by the ſame AUTHOR, *now in the
Preſs for Publication.*

XII. A Tract *on the Law of Nature* and Principles of
Action in Man.

XIII. THE CASE OF SAUL; being an Appendage to
the former Tract, wherein the *compound Nature*
and various *Principles of Action in* MAN (with the
Reality of *ſupernatural ſpiritual Influence*, both *good*
. and *bad)* are proved by unqueſtionable Examples
from the Hiſtory of that unfortunate Monarch, and
alſo from many other Parts of Scripture.

www.ingramcontent.com/pod-product-compliance
Lightning Source LLC
Chambersburg PA
CBHW030720110426
42739CB00030B/1011